HAL•LEONARD®
GUITAR
PLAY-ALONG

AUDIO
ACCESS
INCLUDED

IRON MAIDEN

PLAYBACK+
Speed • Pitch • Balance • Loop

To access audio visit:
www.halleonard.com/mylibrary

Enter Code
8394-7202-0355-7047

Cover photo © Neil Zlozower / Atlasicons.com

ISBN 978-1-4234-9683-0

HAL•LEONARD®
CORPORATION
7777 W. BLUEMOUND RD. P.O. BOX 13819 MILWAUKEE, WI 53213

Visit Hal Leonard Online at
www.halleonard.com

CONTENTS

GUITAR NOTATION LEGEND

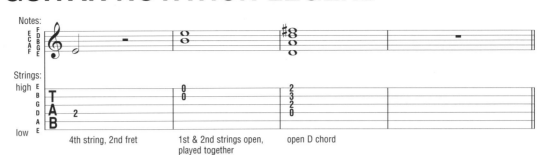

THE MUSICAL STAFF shows pitches and rhythms and is divided by bar lines into measures. Pitches are named after the first seven letters of the alphabet.

TABLATURE graphically represents the guitar fingerboard. Each horizontal line represents a string, and each number represents a fret.

4th string, 2nd fret | 1st & 2nd strings open, played together | open D chord

HALF-STEP BEND: Strike the note and bend up 1/2 step.

WHOLE-STEP BEND: Strike the note and bend up one step.

GRACE NOTE BEND: Strike the note and immediately bend up as indicated.

SLIGHT (MICROTONE) BEND: Strike the note and bend up 1/4 step.

BEND AND RELEASE: Strike the note and bend up as indicated, then release back to the original note. Only the first note is struck.

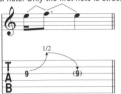

PRE-BEND: Bend the note as indicated, then strike it.

VIBRATO: The string is vibrated by rapidly bending and releasing the note with the fretting hand.

PALM MUTING: The note is partially muted by the pick hand lightly touching the string(s) just before the bridge.

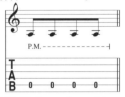

HAMMER-ON: Strike the first (lower) note with one finger, then sound the higher note (on the same string) with another finger by fretting it without picking.

PULL-OFF: Place both fingers on the notes to be sounded. Strike the first note and without picking, pull the finger off to sound the second (lower) note.

LEGATO SLIDE: Strike the first note and then slide the same fret-hand finger up or down to the second note. The second note is not struck.

SHIFT SLIDE: Same as legato slide, except the second note is struck.

TRILL: Very rapidly alternate between the notes indicated by continuously hammering on and pulling off.

TAPPING: Hammer ("tap") the fret indicated with the pick-hand index or middle finger and pull off to the note fretted by the fret hand.

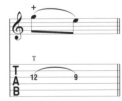

NATURAL HARMONIC: Strike the note while the fret-hand lightly touches the string directly over the fret indicated.

PINCH HARMONIC: The note is fretted normally and a harmonic is produced by adding the edge of the thumb or the tip of the index finger of the pick hand to the normal pick attack.

TREMOLO PICKING: The note is picked as rapidly and continuously as possible.

VIBRATO BAR DIVE AND RETURN: The pitch of the note or chord is dropped a specified number of steps (in rhythm), then returned to the original pitch.

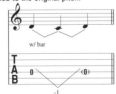

VIBRATO BAR SCOOP: Depress the bar just before striking the note, then quickly release the bar.

VIBRATO BAR DIP: Strike the note and then immediately drop a specified number of steps, then release back to the original pitch.

Additional Musical Definitions

    (accent)   • Accentuate note (play it louder).

    (staccato)   • Play the note short.

D.S. al Coda   • Go back to the sign (%), then play until the measure marked "*To Coda*," then skip to the section labelled "**Coda**."

D.C. al Fine   • Go back to the beginning of the song and play until the measure marked "*Fine*" (end).

Fill   • Label used to identify a brief melodic figure which is to be inserted into the arrangement.

N.C.   • Harmony is implied.

   • Repeat measures between signs.

• When a repeated section has different endings, play the first ending only the first time and the second ending only the second time.

Aces High

Words and Music by Steve Harris

Interlude

Guitar Solo

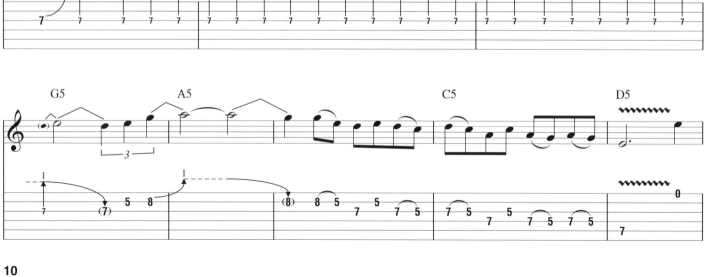

Interlude

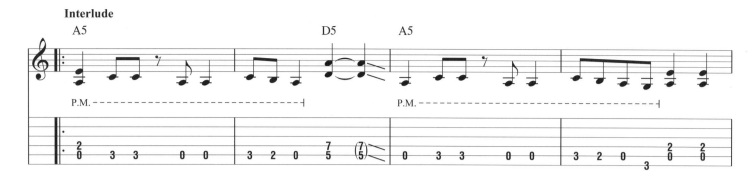

2nd time, D.S. al Coda

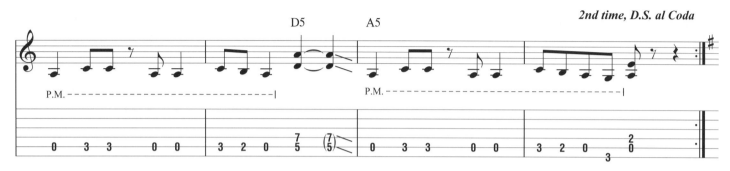

✪ **Coda**

Outro

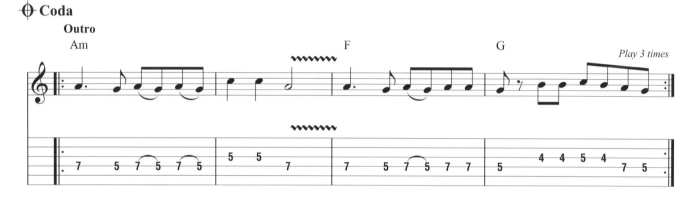

Free time

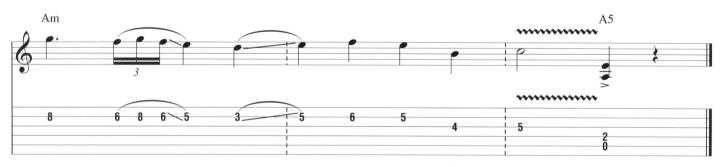

Additional Lyrics

2. Move in to fire at the mainstream of bombers.
   Let off a sharp burst and then turn away.
   Roll over, spin 'round and come in behind them.
   Move to their blindsides and firing again.
   Bandits at eight o'clock move in behind us,
   Ten Me-109s out of the sun.
   Ascending and turning our Spitfires to face them,
   Heading straight for them I press down my guns.

Wasted Years

Words and Music by Adrian Smith

Intro
Moderately ♩ = 150

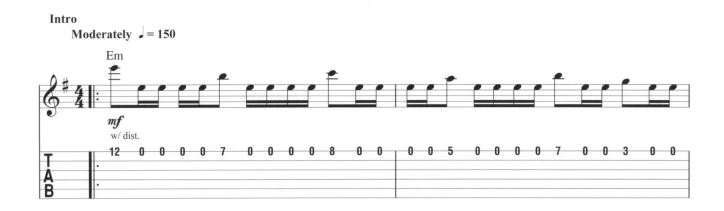

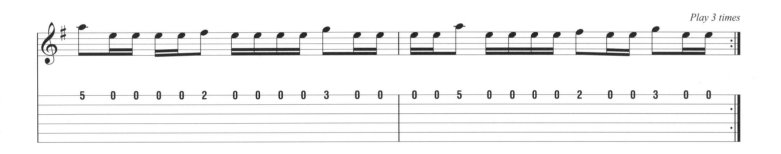

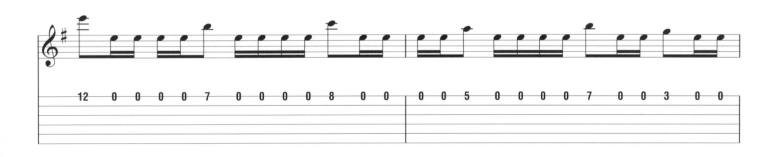

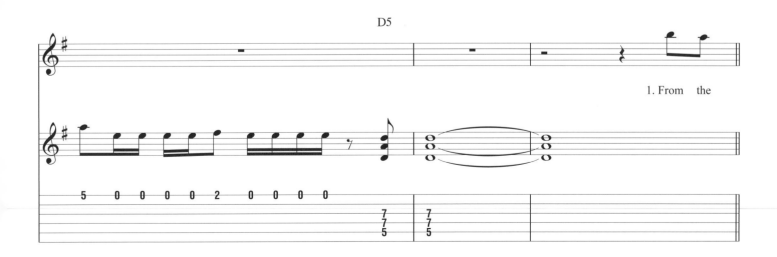

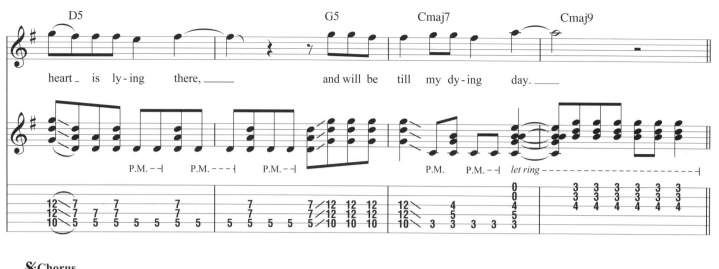

heart _ is ly-ing there, _____ and will be till my dy-ing day. _____

P.M. ⌐ P.M. ---⌐ P.M. ⌐ P.M. P.M. ---⌐ *let ring* -----------------------

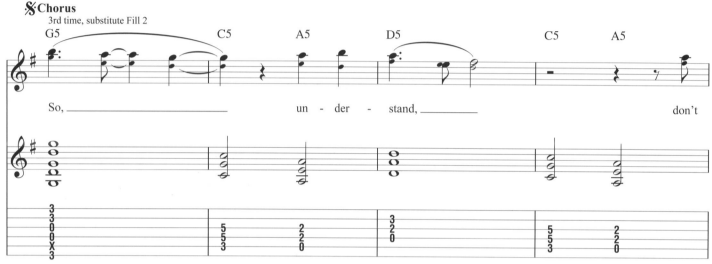

𝄋 Chorus

3rd time, substitute Fill 2

So, _____ un - der - stand, _____ don't

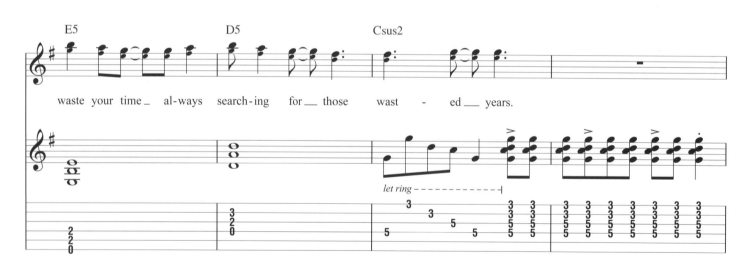

waste your time _ al-ways search-ing for _ those wast - ed _ years.

let ring -------------

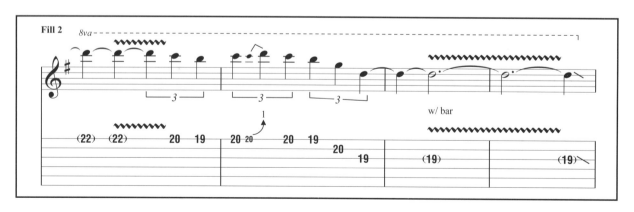

Fill 2

8va ---

w/ bar

Face up, _____ make your stand. _____ And re - al - ize _____ you're

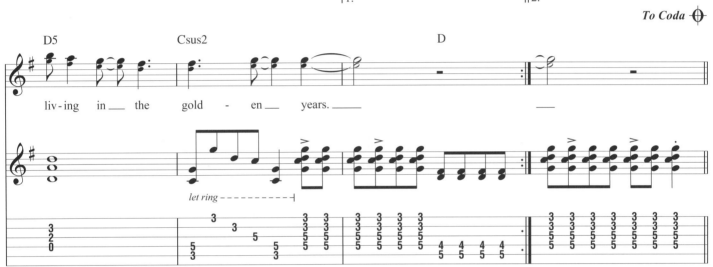

liv-ing in _____ the gold - en _____ years. _____

Interlude

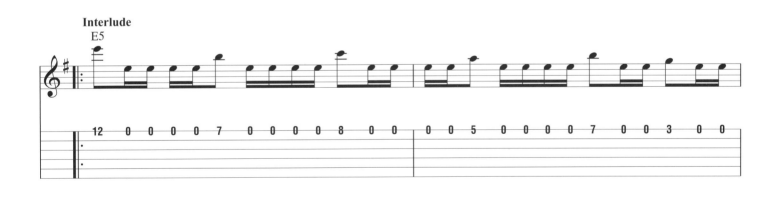

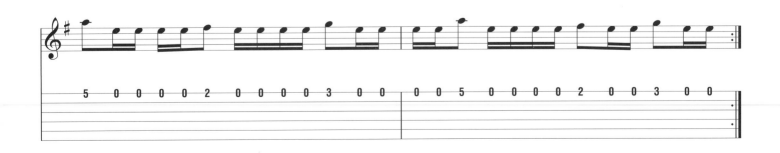

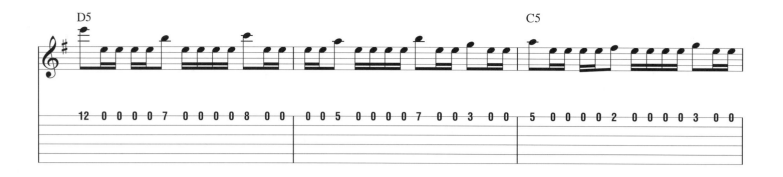

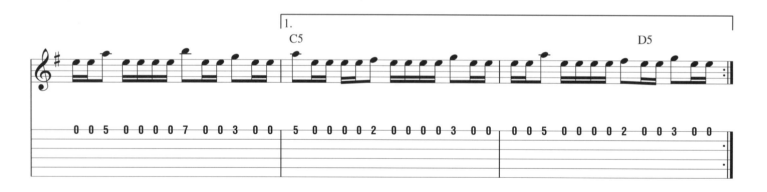

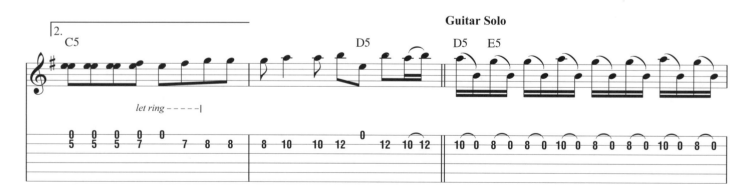

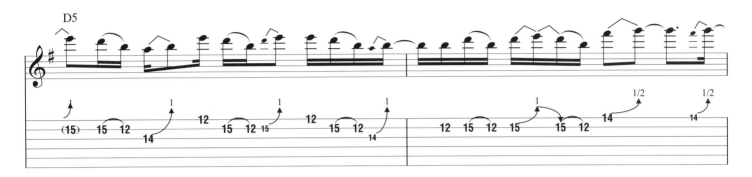

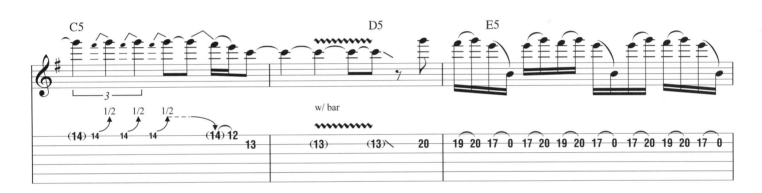

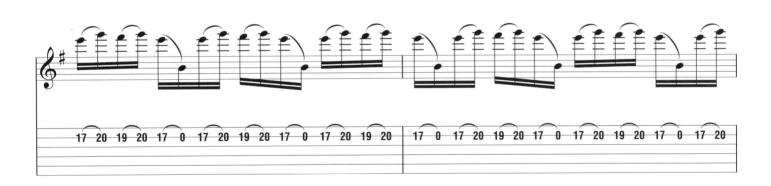

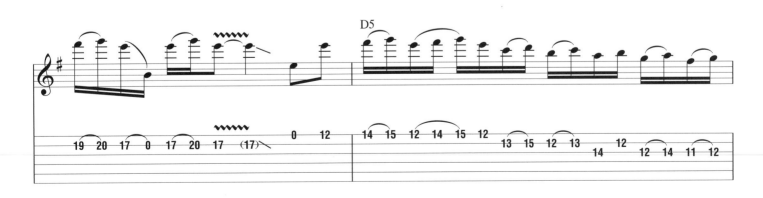

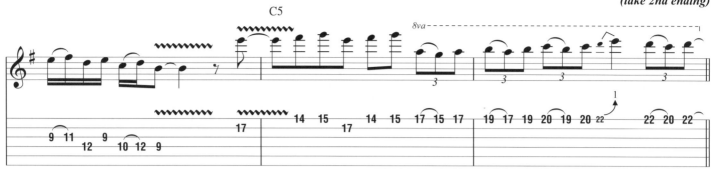

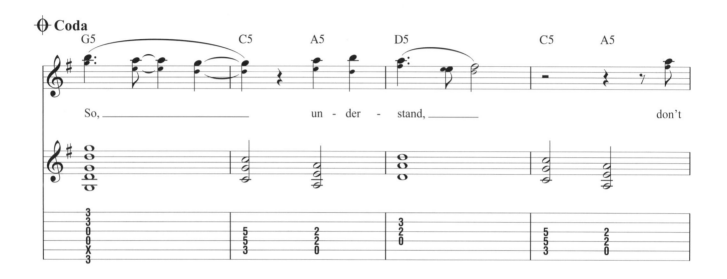

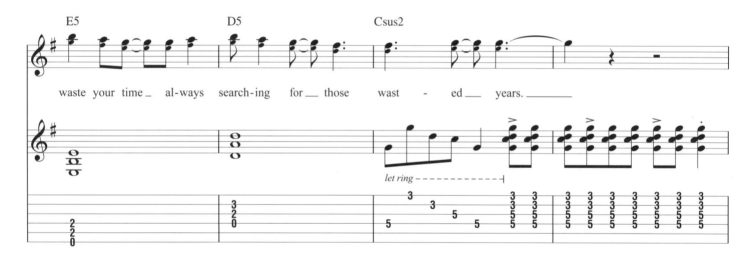

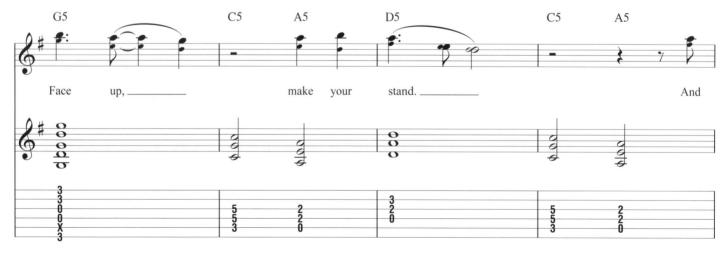

Additional Lyrics

3. Too much time on my hands.
   I've got you on my mind.
   Can't ease this pain so easily.
   When you can't find the words to say,
   It's hard to make it through another day.
   And it makes me want to cry
   And throw my hands up to the sky.

Flight of Icarus

Words and Music by Bruce Dickinson and Adrian Smith

Outro

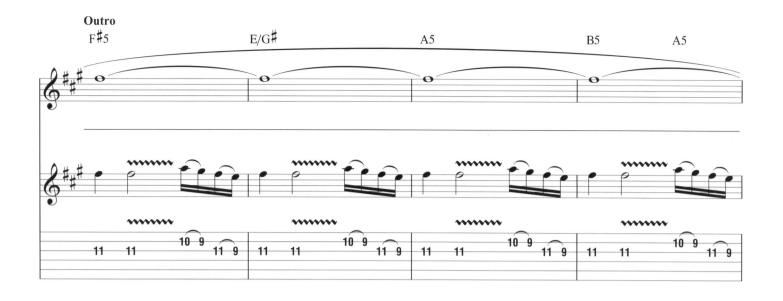

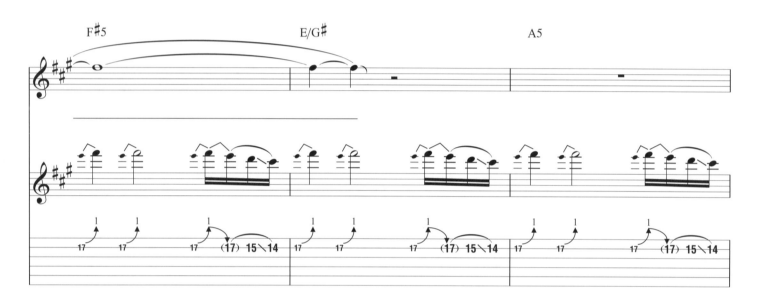

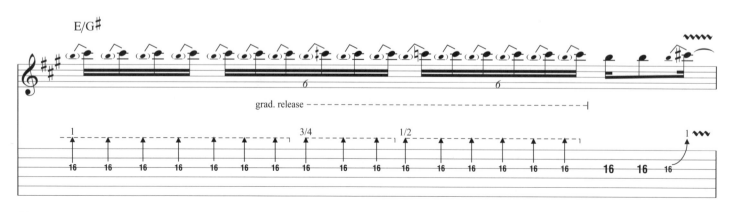

The Number of the Beast

Words and Music by Steve Harris

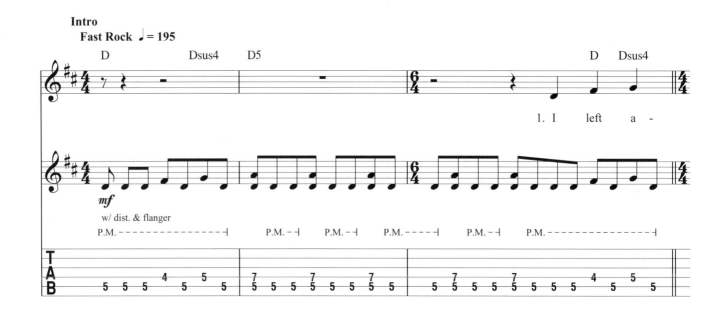

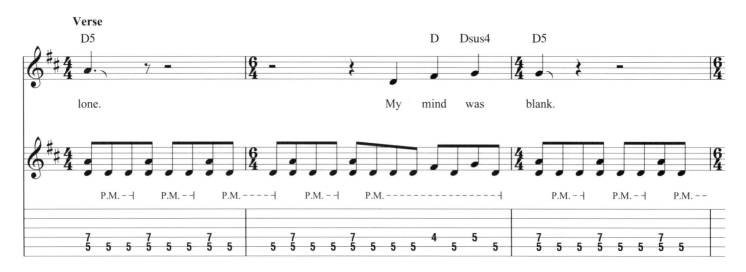

Additional Lyrics

4. Torches blazed and sacred chants were praised
   As they start to cry, hands held to the sky.
   In the night, the fires are burning bright.
   The ritual has begun. Satan's work is done.

5. This can't go on, I must inform the law.
   Can they still be real or just some crazy dream?
   But I feel drawn towards the chanting hordes,
   Seem to mesmerize, can't avoid their eyes.

Run to the Hills

Words and Music by Steve Harris

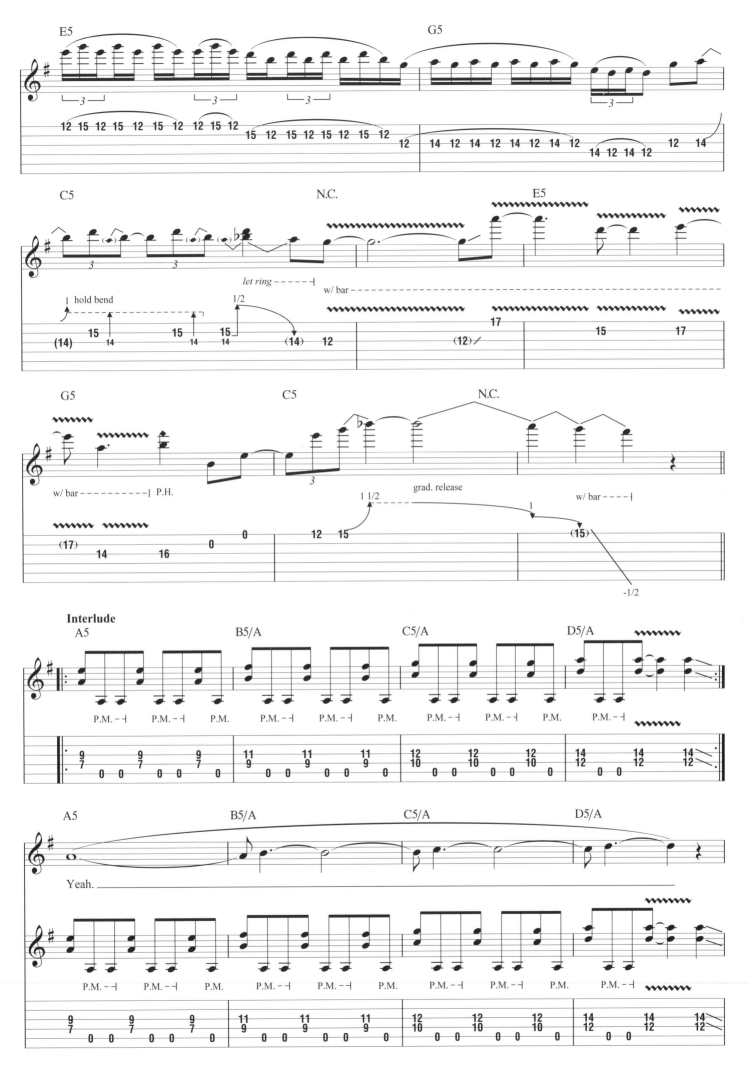

Outro-Chorus

Additional Lyrics

3. Soldier blue in the barren wastes,
   Hunting and killing's a game.
   Raping the women and wasting the men;
   The only good injuns are tame.
   Selling them whiskey and taking their gold,
   Enslaving the young and destroying the old.

Running Free

Words and Music by Steve Harris and Paul Andrews

Coda

Additional Lyrics

2. I spent the night in L.A. jail
   And listened to the sirens wail.
   But they ain't got a thing on me.
   I'm runnin' wild, I'm runnin' free.

3. Pulled her at the Bottle Top,
   A whiskey, dancing, disco hop.
   Now all the boys are after me,
   And that's the way it's gonna be.

The Trooper

Words and Music by Steve Harris

Intro

Moderately fast Rock ♩ = 160

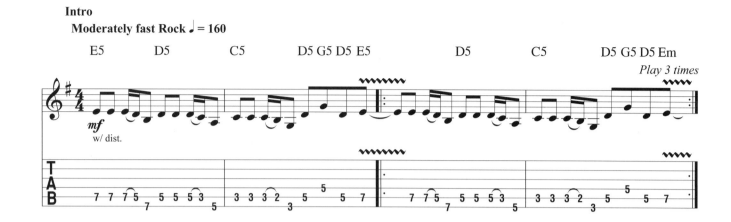

2nd time, substitute Fill 1

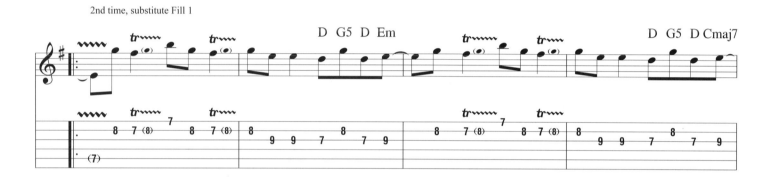

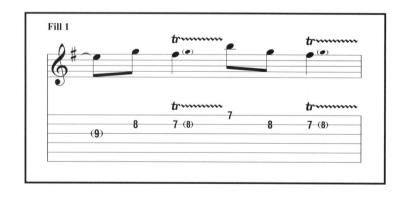

Fill 1

The smell of ac-rid smoke and hors-es' breath __

as I plunge on in-to cer-tain death. Oh. __

Chorus

2nd time, substitute Fill 2

Fill 2

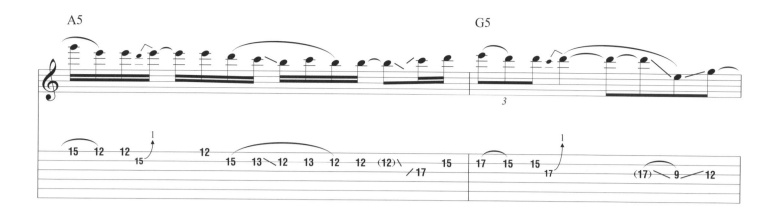

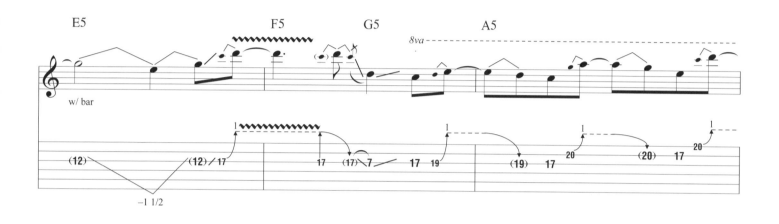

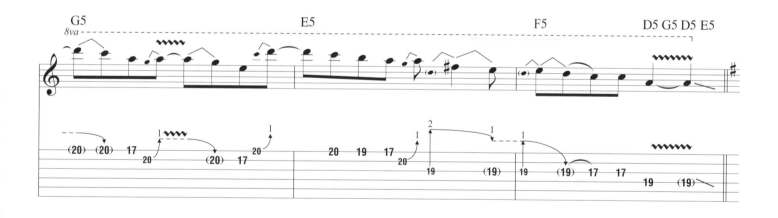

Interlude

2nd time, substitute Fill 1

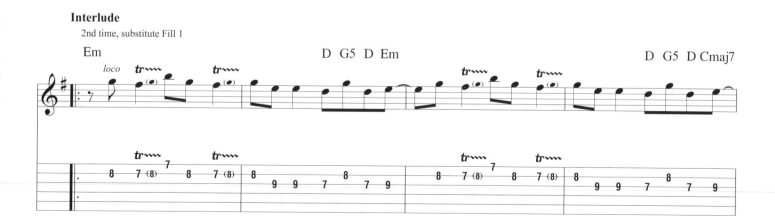

Outro

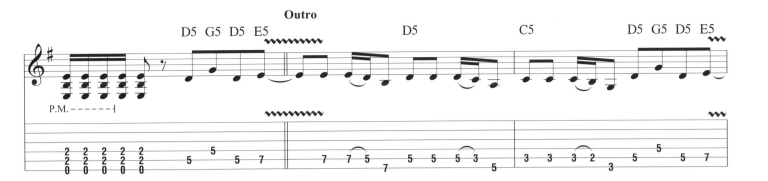

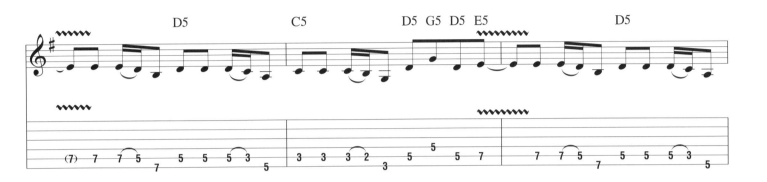

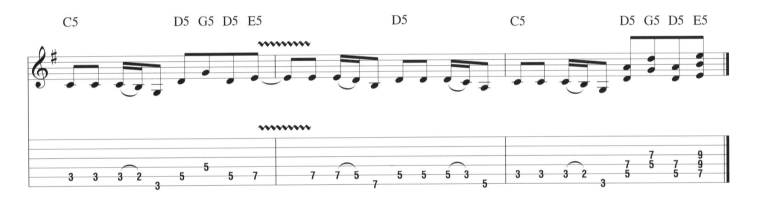

Additional Lyrics

3. We get so close, near enough to fight,
When a Russian gets me in his sights.
He pulls the trigger and I feel the blow,
A burst of rounds takes my horse below.
And as I lay there gazing at the sky,
My body's numb and my throut is dry.
And as I lay forgotten and alone,
Without a tear I draw my parting groan.

Two Minutes to Midnight

Words and Music by Bruce Dickinson and Adrian Smith

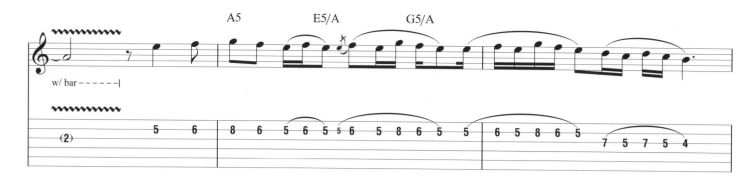

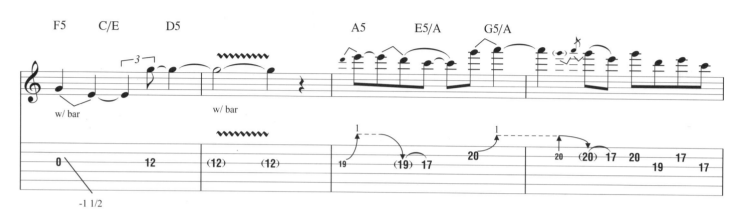

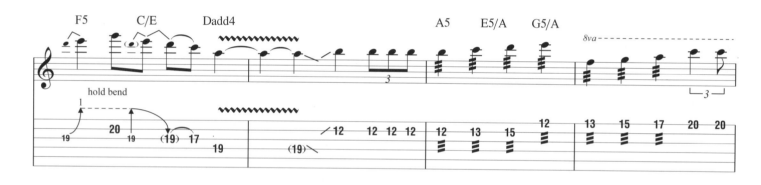

Guitar Solo
Half-time feel

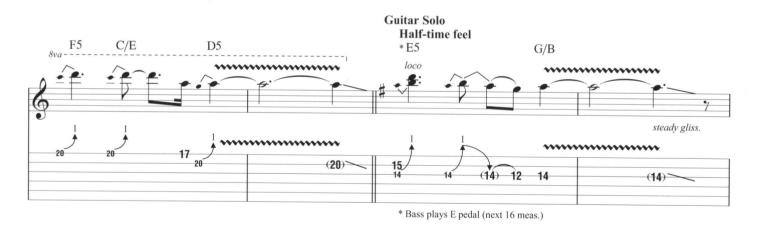

* Bass plays E pedal (next 16 meas.)

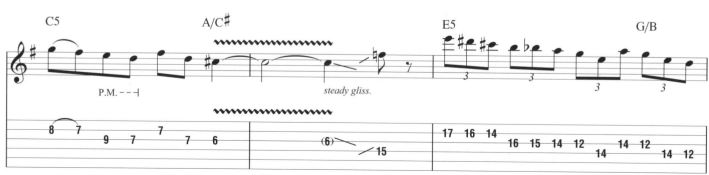